YOUR MUSIC AND PEOPLE

YOUR MUSIC AND PEOPLE

creative and considerate fame

DEREK SIVERS

HIT MEDIA
New York, New York

Designer: Helen Robinson
Editor: Aly Tadros
Producer: Saeah Lee Wood

Go to *sive.rs/m* for quantity sales, special discounts,
and custom dedications directly from the author.

Hit Media
212 Park Avenue
New York, New York
hitmedia.com

Contents

PEOPLE

INDUSTRY

Resourceful

Describe

Target

Quantity

Money

Mindset

INTRO

What's inside this book

Welcome to my book about getting your music to people, into people, and through people.

You deserve a little preview of what's inside, so I'm going to introduce you to all of its main ideas, right now, all at once. It'll be a bunch of declarations in a row, like reading a table of contents, but it'll give you an idea of what's to come. Ready?

- Marketing is an extension of your art. Business is just as creative as music.

- Marketing means being considerate. Focus on others. See yourself from their point of view. Being weird is considerate.

- All opportunities come from people. Stay in touch with everyone. Use a database.

- People skills are counterintuitive. To be helped, be helpful. Persistence is polite.

- Be resourceful. Ask for help, but never wait for help. Call the destination and ask for directions. Get specific about what you want.

- The music industry is run by cool people like you. Don't put them on a pedestal.

- Describe your music in a curious way, and it will travel faster and further.

- Be extreme and sharply defined. Target a niche. Proudly exclude most people.

- Money is just a neutral representation of value. Be valuable to others—not just yourself. People like to pay.

- Decide if you're at the starting line or finish line. Nobody knows the future, so focus on what doesn't change.

- Whatever scares you, go do it.

That's it! That's the whole book. These 88 tiny chapters will explain these points.

At the end of each one, I'll give you the web address of that chapter, where you can read the interesting comments or questions people have about it.

When you're done reading this book, please email me to let me know. Anyone who finishes this book is my kind of person, so please introduce yourself and feel free to email me any questions. All of my contact info is at **sive.rs.**

SOME QUICK CONTEXT FOR THESE STORIES

This book is entirely about you and your music. But I use some of my stories as examples. So here's my context, as short as can be, to set the stage for the book.

Since I was 14, all I wanted was to be a successful musician.

First I graduated from Berklee College of Music in Boston.

Then I got a job at Warner/Chappell Music Publishing in New York City. There I learned a ton about how the traditional music industry works. I'll tell you about that soon.

Then I quit my job and became a full-time professional musician. I played over a thousand shows of all types. I was also a session guitarist and side-man, then I ran a recording studio, booking agency, record label, and more.

I made a website to sell my CD, then my musician friends asked if I could sell their CD too. So I called it CD Baby, and it soon became the largest seller of independent music online. Over 150,000 musicians sold their music directly through me. (I have a different book about that, called "Anything You Want".)

I started to see the music business from the other side. I found out what it was like to be on the receiving end of musicians' music. I became friends with successful people inside the music industry, and heard their perspective.

I saw thousands of musicians succeed. So I paid attention to how they did it.

That's when I started writing my observations in this book. I felt like a spy, giving you the report from the inside, telling you how to get in.

Now listen up, and I'll tell you everything I know.

CREATIVE

Art doesn't end at the edge of the canvas

Imagine you see a caged feather on a museum wall. The sign underneath says the artist is a political activist in jail.

Imagine that same caged feather again. But instead the sign says the artist is a high school kid in Florida.

Or imagine that the only way to see it is to crawl deep into a shrinking tunnel that opens into a room of mirrors, where the caged feather is suspended by a thread.

Same feather. Very different perceptions.

The way you present your art, and what people know about it, completely changes how they perceive it.

Therefore, your art doesn't end at the edge of the canvas. Your creative decisions continue all the way to the end.

Now think of the way you create and release music:

- You have a tiny idea for a song.

- You flesh it out into a full song.

- You give it layers of instruments.

- You choose its texture when recording.

- You come up with an album title, and the visual look of your photos and videos.

Every step so far has been a creative expansion of your original idea.

So now it's time to put it out into the world. **Do you turn off all that creativity?** Just upload the song to the usual places, and announce it like everyone else?

No! Your creative process hasn't stopped! Flaunt your artistic freedoms, and have some fun with it!

- the way you communicate with the world

- how you make your music available

- the stories you tell about your music and yourself

These are all the continuation of your creation.

Marketing is the final extension of your art.

Business is creative

A famous record label executive was confronted by a musician who said, "You don't value creativity!" The executive said, "Oh please! I've got accountants more creative than you!"

It's meant as an insult, but it has a point. Don't think of music as creative but business as not. Business is definitely just as creative as music.

Most musicians are wildly creative when writing, playing, performing, and recording. But as soon as it's time to do business, they stiffen up and lose their confidence. They follow advice that tells them exactly how to promote.

But turning off your creativity—trying to play it safe—is the worst thing you could do. Just like with music.

So loosen up! Get confident, creative, playful, and experimental. Break the rules. **Try some things that nobody else has done.**

Think of how comfortable you are on your instrument—improvising, experimenting, and having fun with it.

Now be that comfortable when marketing. Improvise. Experiment. And have fun with it!

This is only a test.
See what happens

In America in the 1970s, they would test the Emergency Broadcast System on TV, with a long "BEEEEEEP". At the end, an announcer would say, "This is a test. This is only a test."

That phrase is burned into my brain. "This is a test. This is only a test." It's very useful to remember when pursuing your career.

Everything usually feels so serious—like if you make one mistake, it'll all end in disaster. But really everything you do is just a test: an experiment to **see what happens.**

My favorite times in life started with a "see what happens" approach.

Let's see what happens if I run my vocals through my guitar pedals.

Let's see what happens if I invite that famous producer out to lunch.

Let's see what happens if I call that radio station to ask their advice.

It's actually impossible to fail if your only mission was to see what happens!

"This is a test. This is only a test." There is no downside. Try everything!

Restrictions will set you free

Someone says, "Write me a piece of music. Anything. No restrictions. Go!"

You're stumped. It's the blank page syndrome.

Instead, someone says, "Write me a piece of music using only a flute, ukulele, and this toy piano. You can only use the notes D, E, and B. It has to start quiet, get louder, then end quietly. Go!"

Aha! Now that's an inspiring challenge!

You can use this approach for business, too. **If you're feeling stuck with marketing, give yourself restrictions.**

- Contact fifty fans using only personal emails—no mass-mailing.

- Make a music video using only stock footage.

- Give promotion a time-limit of just 15 minutes per day.

- Spend a week only contacting people you've never contacted before.

Whenever you're feeling uninspired or unmotivated, use creative restrictions to set you free.

Make mystery: make people wonder

Do you remember when you first started listening to music? It was all so mysterious, as you wondered what those lyrics meant or how they made those sounds.

Try to create that feeling for your audience.

Don't be so plain or obvious that there's nothing left to wonder. But don't be so cryptic that they give up.

Use obscure references in your lyrics. Produce unusual sounds in your recording. Make strange images in your photos and videos.

Give just enough to make them curious. Let them search for explanations, clues, or context.

Keith Richards of the Rolling Stones said he tries to write lyrics that are like listening in to someone else's phone conversation—where you don't know the context and don't get the references, so it draws you in deeper, trying to understand. To do this, he first writes down everything he wants to say, then he crosses out every other line, and writes the song using only what's left.

Maybe due to social media, artists are less mysterious than ever. It's kind of sad to have everything so transparent. **Once something is explained, it stops captivating your curiosity.**

There was an interesting psychology experiment. Many people were given a trivial quiz. Before they began, they could choose what reward to receive when finished: either the answers to the quiz, or a chocolate bar. Almost everyone chose the chocolate bar. But after taking the quiz, they were given one last chance to choose their reward: either the answers to those questions, or the chocolate bar. Almost everyone changed their mind, and now preferred to know the answers.

Once people start wondering, they can't stand not knowing.

Make mystery in and around your music.

Creative communication

The way you communicate with people is part of your art.

For people who have never heard your music, it's the *start* of your art!

If you make depressing music, send your fans a dark black announcement that's depressing just to look at.

If you are an "in-your-face country-metal-speedpunk" artist, have the guts to call a potential booking agent and scream, "Listen you crazy dirtbag! Book me or I explode! Waaaaaah!!" If they like that introduction, you've found a good match.

Set the tone. Pull in those people who love that kind of thing. Proudly alienate those that don't.

There's a minimalist classical music composer whose emails to me are always just one provocative thought. Like when I posted something online about being an introvert, he emailed me just one sentence: "Are we not ever-changing, both gradually and per situation?" That's it. No greeting or closing or manners in-between. His communication style always makes me smile, and reminds me of his music.

The gentle new-age artist always calls me "sweetie" and reminds me to nourish my soul

The surf-music artist always uses the Hawaiian greetings "aloha" and "mahalo" when he emails, along with other surfer slang.

The rebellious punk never calls me by my name, but instead just says, "Hey sellout."

Be different. **Show who you are.**

It gives people's lives more variety, too.

Captain T

Back in 1997, when "The X Files" was still on the air, a friend of mine who called himself Captain T recorded an album that was all about conspiracy theories, Area 51, and aliens. It was intentionally funny, but he stayed in character. He acted like a guy who was trying to tell the world about government cover-ups.

We wanted to send his album to college radio stations, but couldn't afford to hire a real radio promoter, so we decided to do it ourselves. **We decided to make his marketing an extension of his art and image.**

I had visited many college radio stations and saw that the kids there would receive twenty packages a day, all exactly the same, in the same boring envelopes, with a little cover letter saying the same thing: "Please consider this album for airplay." **I wanted to be considerate and give them something different.**

So we bought 500 black envelopes, 500 sheets of brown paper, 500 alien head stickers, and 500 huge red labels that said "CONFIDENTIAL! DO NOT OPEN FOR ANY REASON".

We did a mail-merge to the 500 program directors at 500 college radio stations, so that each one got a personalized printed letter that said this:

> Dear _____,
>
> You don't know me, but I live in the bushes behind your station.
>
> I have been here for 12 years, and your station has saved my life many times over.

The music that you play has kept me going through my darkest of days and for this I owe you everything.

So I must tell you that a man named Captain T found me in the gutter yesterday, and he taught me about what is really going on with the government cover-ups, and what really happened down there in Area 51 with the aliens. This man has a message that you have to get out to the world, because people need to know the truth!!!

Signed,
The man in the bushes, looking through your window right now.

We took each letter out to the backyard and rubbed it in dirt, then crumpled it up. Then we put the crumpled letter and CD into each black envelope, sealed it with an alien head sticker, and finally covered it with the huge label that said "CONFIDENTIAL! DO NOT OPEN FOR ANY REASON". And that's what we mailed to each radio station.

Now imagine you're that college kid receiving twenty boring packages per day. Then you get this scary black package that says "DO NOT OPEN". When you open it, it's covered in dirt and says, "You don't know me, but I live in the bushes behind your station."

375 of the 500 radio stations played it.

Every now and then, my friend Captain T gets approached by someone that used to work at a college radio station back in 1997. They tell him they still remember it, because it was the coolest package they ever got.

CONSIDERATE

"Marketing" just means being considerate

Don't confuse the word "marketing" with advertising, announcing, spamming, or giving away branded crap.

Really, "marketing" just means being considerate.

Marketing means making it easy for people to notice you, relate to you, remember you, and tell their friends about you.

Marketing means listening for what people need, and creating something surprisingly tailored for them.

Marketing means getting to know people, making a deeper connection, and keeping in touch.

All of these are just considerate—looking at things from the other person's point of view, and doing what's best for them.

A lot of musicians say, "I hate marketing!" So, yeah, if you thought marketing meant turning off your creativity, spending lots of money, and being annoying, then it's a good thing you don't like that. Nobody likes that.

Just find creative ways to be considerate. That's the best marketing.

It's hard to get off stage

Being a songwriter is weird. You dig deep inside yourself. You extract and explain your emotions. Then you broadcast your innermost feelings to the biggest possible audience.

It's a life that demands a deep focus on yourself. It's all you, you, you. It's a one-way road that goes from inside of you out to the audience.

Because of this, it's hard for you to turn that off, switch directions, and just listen to others.

The essence of marketing is looking at everything from the other person's point of view. So it's no surprise that musicians find it hard to switch into that mode.

It's OK. Have some compassion for your situation. It's a side-effect of the craft. Don't beat yourself up over it.

But first, before you begin marketing, get off the stage. Pause your habit of broadcasting. Turn the spotlight on your audience. And get ready to listen.

Constantly ask what they really want

This may sound obvious, but for me it made all the difference.

Before I interact with people, I ask myself this question: "What do they really want?"

Like if I'm writing someone an email, I ask, "Why are they really reading this email?"

If I'm contacting an agent, I ask, "Why are they really doing this job?"

If I'm about to perform a show, I ask, "What are they really hoping to get from a night out at a concert?"

Thinking of everything from the other person's point of view is one of the best things you can do in life.

Be what they want. And maybe they'll be what you want, too.

Don't try to sound big

When communicating with your fans and contacts, don't try to sound bigger than you are.

Don't use the corporate "we". Say "I". Fans want to connect with you as a person, not as a brand.

Don't appear flawless. Show a charming flaw. Confidence attracts, but vulnerability endears.

Definitely don't use corporate-speak to try to sound like you're a big business. It comes across as fake, insecure, or spam.

Your fans are your friends. Speak to them like real people. Be weird. **Prove you're a real person.** Write every post or email as if it was from you to your best friend.

People have grown deaf to the bland language of big business. It all sounds like contrived posturing. It has no personality—no voice.

This is one reason why it's so much cooler to be small and independent instead of big and corporate.

Being able to say "I" in your communication with fans is a great competitive advantage.

Considerate communication

You get a big long email from someone and think, "Ooof. I'll come back to that later." (Then you never do.)

Someone tries to contact you using a technology you hate, like a surprising incoming video call.

You have a dilemma and need a good conversation, so you reach out to someone who replies, "Can you make it quick?"

You're overwhelmed with work on a tight deadline, and a friend calls trying to have a long conversation.

It's hard to match your communication with someone else's preference and situation.

There's a huge benefit to having a great conversation, but sometimes you need to be extremely succinct. So how do you reconcile this? Here's my advice:

First, prepare the most succinct version of your reason for contacting someone. Make it so short that if the person only has 30 seconds to talk, you could communicate your point, ask your question, and get the answer.

With real-time communication, like text or phone, just start by asking if they have time. If they do, then take the time to get personal, be a friend, and have a good conversation. But if they don't, then just use the short version.

With non-real-time communication, like email, assume you've only got ten seconds. **Edit your emails down to a few sentences.** But always give a link to more information, so they can check it out if they have time. And include your other contact information, in case they prefer a longer conversation about it. (This is what email signatures are for.) Then, if they reply and ask, you can give the extra information you left out before.

Some hate texting. Some hate calls. Some hate video. Some hate it all. Just keep track of their preference for future use.

This may sound obvious, but it's a bigger problem than people realize. Considerate communication is surprisingly rare.

Touch as many of their senses as you can

The more senses you touch in someone, the more they'll remember you.

The most sensory experience is a live show, with you sweating in front of them, the sound system pounding their chest, the flashing lights, the smell of the stinky club, and the visceral feeling of pushing up against strangers.

The least sensory experience is an email or a plain web page.

Reach as many senses as possible.

- Have some great photos that you use next to any text.

- Make a video for every song.

- Be a guest on every video-show you can.

- At your live shows, burn incense or hug every person there, or…

You get the idea. **Keep aiming for the most sensory way to reach your audience.**

LIFE IS LIKE HIGH SCHOOL

When you're in high school, it's all about popularity, cliques, and being cool.

When you go to college, the focus shifts to academic achievement.

Many people get out of college thinking the world will be like that—like the harder you work, the more you'll be rewarded. But it's not.

Life is like high school. It's all about how you come across, how social you are, what scene you're in, being likeable, and being cool.

But you can make this work in your favor.

You can be your idealized self.

You can be where things are happening.

You can attend cool events, and invite people to join you.

You can practice your social skills and be the kind of person that people like to help.

You can approach this strategically, as if you were a new kid going to a new school, with a goal to be popular. It sounds shallow, but it works.

Be who they want to be. In your role as a musician, it's actually considerate!

It'd be easier to put in no effort and be normal. Show up wearing whatever, take a normal photo, and be a regular person.

But people want someone to look up to. Someone who's not of their normal boring world. Someone who's being who they wish they could be, if they had the courage.

It takes some extra effort to look and act cool instead of normal, but it's considerate and part of your art.

Look back at artists like Andy Warhol or Miles Davis, who were not only great at their art, but also knew how to play their image—to be cool.

Barking

I'm in New York City. Across the street is a man pacing on the sidewalk. He's insanely barking something at the top of his lungs. Everyone is avoiding going anywhere near him.

I get closer. I try to figure out what he's screaming about. Finally I hear it. "20% coupons for window shades! 20% off! Window shades! Get your coupons here!"

Yeah… uh… that's not working.

A week later, I'm hanging with a friend in Union Square. The whole time we're talking, there's some man yelling in the background. It's almost like he's singing a repetitive phrase—always an F falling to a D. Again I'm curious, so I get closer to hear what he's yelling. "Help feed the homeless! Help feed the homeless!"

Ah! So he's trying to help! But again, everyone is avoiding him.

Then it made me think: **How many of us do this?**

Maybe we weren't getting the results we wanted, so we thought if we shouted louder, more people would hear.

But people avoid those types. If someone always pitches his business to friends at parties, he won't get invited to parties anymore.

In England, I heard the word "barking" used as slang for "insane". (It's short for "barking mad", get it?)

When promoting, make sure you're not barking.

When things aren't working, be smarter, not louder.

PEOPLE

Get personal

Before I got into the music industry, I had an idea of what it would look like: Some powerful manager or agent calling me into his office to discuss the business of my music.

Then I moved to New York City and became friends with cool people who also did things in music. Sometimes these people were agents or managers, but that was secondary. Mostly we were just friends.

Sometimes I'd send them clients. Sometimes they'd hook me up with opportunities. But really we were just friends, talking about our love lives or ideas, hanging out and having fun.

It was a long time before I realized that I was already in the industry—that this is how things are done. **People send business to people they like.** It's all more personal than I had expected.

One of my best friends in the world is also my lawyer. He's one of the top music lawyers in the world, but mostly he's my friend. We talk about cycling, his kids, and music. And sometimes we stop to discuss a recent contract.

The initial contact usually happens for professional reasons. Like when I was looking for a lawyer, and someone introduced me to this guy.

When I hear music I love, I contact the musician, and say let's meet. Within minutes we're talking about her dogs, microphones, Japan, and whatever. Then, when someone asks me to recommend some music, guess who comes to mind first?

Point is: As you're out there in the music business, get personal.

Don't always be selling yourself. That keeps people at a distance from you, because it shows you're not friends.

Even if it starts professional, get personal as soon as possible. Be a friend. That's how things are done.

Always think how you can help someone

When someone says they're looking for something, remember it, and help them find it. Introduce people to each other.

Also listen carefully for what they might not realize they need.

Ask them what's the hardest part about their job. People love to complain. And each complaint gives you an idea about how you could help.

When you come across something that might be useful, go through the list of everyone you know, and think if it's particularly useful to that person. If so, contact them personally to tell them about it. Not a mass blast, but a real just-to-you recommendation. That's much more meaningful because it shows you were thinking of them in particular.

There's always a favor you can do. **Give give give, and sometimes you will receive.**

Don't be afraid to ask for favors

Have you ever asked for directions in a city? People get a little ego boost when they know the answer to something you're asking. They'll gladly show off their knowledge.

So don't be afraid to ask for favors. **People like doing favors!**

When I lived in New York City, one bold musician I know called me and said, "I'm coming to New York in two months. Can you give me a list of all the important contacts you think I should meet?" I laughed because I admired his directness! Then I emailed him a list of twenty people he should call.

Sometimes you need to find something specific: a video director, a JavaScript programmer, a sitar player. Contact everyone you know and ask. Friends of friends will know how to get everything you want in life.

Some people have time on their hands and would rather help you do something interesting instead of watching TV. Need help doing promotion? Need help getting equipment to a show? **Just ask them!**

By making them feel important, connected, and needed, you'll be doing them a favor, too.

Small gifts go a long way

When I worked at Warner/Chappell, I was the least-important person in the company, just working in the library.

Since it's the largest music publisher in the world, I dealt with hundreds of people. I can't remember most of their names. But three times, and only three times, I got a surprise gift from one of our songwriters.

1. James Mastro, from The Bongos, got me a cool little "Mother Mary" keychain when he toured Spain.

2. Gerry DeVeaux, the multi-platinum dance writer, got me some funky plastic fish Christmas ornaments when he went to the Bahamas.

3. And Jane Kelly Williams got me a red sweatshirt.

Can you believe I remember these details twenty years later? Believe it!

If any of these three people asked me for a favor, I'd be sure to help them out.

As you climb the ladder of success, giving a gift may go a long way and be remembered for years.

Get presents for the people you've met that are probably under-appreciated. Don't waste gifts on the high-power people. They already receive too many.

Be generous. You're going to see the same faces for years to come.

Persistence is polite

As teenagers, we learned the hard way that if you contact someone and they don't reply, they're just not into you. If you keep trying, you must be a total loser.

But in the business world, it's the opposite. **If you don't keep trying, you're a loser!**

If someone doesn't get back to you, it probably wasn't intentional. Everyone is busy, and their situation has nothing to do with you.

Imagine two different scenarios:

1. Someone doesn't reply, so you get upset and decide they're evil and clearly meant to insult you. You resent them for life, and speak poorly of them forever.

2. Someone doesn't reply, so you assume they must be swamped in work. You wait a week, and contact them again. If still no reply, you feel sympathy that they must be really overwhelmed. You wait a week, and try again. If still no reply, you try to reach them a different way.

Now, which one was rude, and which one was polite?

Repeatedly follow-up
to show you care

I knew a music publicist in New York City when she was at the peak of her success. A few of her clients had hits, so everyone wanted to work with her. She was flooded with new music.

Here's how she dealt with the flood:

Whenever someone sent their music, it would go into an inbox. That inbox was completely ignored.

Whenever someone contacted her to follow-up the first time, to ask if she'd received it, she would take their music out of that first inbox, and put it in a second inbox. That second inbox was also ignored.

Then if they followed-up with her a second time, asking again if she'd had the chance to listen, she would take their music out of the second inbox, and put it in a third inbox. That third inbox would get a listen if she had some spare time.

Finally, if they followed-up a third time, she would take their music out of the third inbox, and make it a priority to give it a real listen.

She saw the shocked look on my face, as she described her system. So she explained:

"I can't listen to everyone, so I can't know who's got the best music. But the ones who follow-up show they've got the tenacity and drive to succeed. As long as their music is also good, then those are the ones I want to work with."

It wasn't ego. It was just a practical way to deal with a flood, and a pretty good filter for choosing new clients.

Maybe nobody else has an official system like this. But un-officially, they do. **Overwhelmed people don't have time for all the random first-contacts.** Patience and persistence separate you from the rest, and show how much you care.

Pedestals prevent friendships

I was a struggling musician, with big ambitions but not much success, when I went to a music industry conference in Las Vegas to promote my music.

I was nervous, but doing everything I could to make connections with the managers at all the big music companies. I attended every panel of experts, noting everyone's name, and approaching the stage afterwards to introduce myself. **I had these people up on a pedestal. I was terrified of them.** The stakes were high. These were the people who could make my career. It was mentally and emotionally exhausting.

So during lunch I went out to the pool and stuck my feet in the water, just to silently retreat. Some dude sat next to me and did the same. He said, "I see you've noticed the bikini girls, too." I had. So we sat there, feet in the pool, talking about those girls over there, how weird Las Vegas is, how his friend was up all night gambling, and other random chit-chat. He was a really cool dude—the rare kind I just click with right away. I assumed he must be a fellow musician.

But when he got up to leave, he said, "Really great talking with you. Let's keep in touch," and handed me his business card. Holy shit! He was the vice president of one of the biggest record labels!

I learned a huge lesson that day.

If I would have known who he was in advance, I never would have had a real conversation with him. I would have been awkward and self-conscious, trying to promote myself. But because I didn't know, I could connect on a personal level, and be a real friend.

I used to think that having connections in the music industry meant that you'd have business meetings, and only talk about your mutual business interests. But again and again I've realized that we make real connections by talking about anything else, and just clicking as friends. **People send business to people they like.**

So beware of putting people on a pedestal. It can prevent a real friendship.

Postscript to this story: We kept in touch, and he ended up sending me some of my most successful CD Baby clients. Now, twenty years later, I just emailed him to tell him I'm writing this story.

INDUSTRY

It's just people inside the machine!

All those years I was trying to get famous, it felt like the music industry was this giant mysterious machine.

I'd submit my music to showcases, and the machine would choose everyone else.

I'd try to contact record labels, and the machine wouldn't let me past the gate.

I'd send my music to media outlets, and the machine would make it disappear.

What a heartless machine! It felt like a complex puzzle that, if I was smart enough, I could figure out.

But then, at age 20, I got a job inside the machine.

Now I was given all-access. I was treated as an insider and invited to all events. I talked with rock stars and their managers. I watched how people got in and how deals get made.

The big epiphany came just a few weeks into the job.

I had to call a major record label to get a copy of a new album. They put me on the phone with Stacy, who ran promotions out of their New York office. She was super-friendly, joking around on the phone, so we decided to meet up for lunch.

She was a bubbly 24-year-old that was a huge music fan, had a degree in media studies, got this job as an intern, climbed the ranks a bit, and was now in charge of promotion.

And that's when it hit me:

This whole music industry—this giant mysterious machine—is not a machine! It's just people!

More specifically, it's mostly young people like Stacy, who have a lot in common with us musicians, and are totally cool and approachable.

So it's not heartless. **We just need to understand what it's like to be them.**

Once I connected with them as people—getting to know them and assuming they mean well—the machine started working for me.

How to get through the gates?

As a young musician, I always heard that you had to get your music "solicited" to the major labels. I never really understood what "solicited" meant, until I worked on the inside. Here's how it actually looks:

Every day, tons of music is sent to the labels from total strangers. It's just too much to deal with, so it's all ignored. All of it.

These companies don't exist to find new music. Their job is to profit from their existing artists. That's a huge job, in itself.

When the manager or lawyer or producer of one of their artists comes in for a meeting, he'll say, "I'm working with this new artist that you need to hear before we head out for lunch." Then the executive will sit and give it a real listen.

And that's how you get heard. **That's what "solicited" means.**

When you send your music unsolicited to some company, you won't get a real listen. Their lack of response says, "Sorry. You don't get it. That's not the way in."

Do your research to find those managers, lawyers, agents, and producers that are already in.

Same thing goes for approaching any too-public target, whether it's a celebrity, or major media outlet, or whatever. **Getting "solicited" through an existing contact is the best way to get through the gates.**

You have to see it from their point of view. Understand what it's like to be overwhelmed with new music. All they can handle is the stuff that's been pre-approved by their trusted contacts.

HAVE SOMEONE WORK THE INSIDE OF THE INDUSTRY

Moby, the famous techno artist, was interviewed by a journalist who said, "I've known you since your early days, and we both know that there were many amazing artists in your scene. So why did you get so much more successful than them?"

Moby said, "While they were pasting up flyers to promote their next gig, I just put that same amount of energy into finding a great team: a manager, agent, publicist, and label. Then, while other musicians just kept gigging, **my career took off because of my team.**"

This came up again when I read the biography of the band U2. After their first hit, they encountered this band in Boston that had been gigging relentlessly for ten years. The guitarist said sadly, "One song on the radio does more for your career than ten years of gigs."

You can write a hundred songs. You can do a thousand gigs. You can have a million followers. **But it won't get you as far as having someone work the inside of the industry.**

Finding your team is hard, but no harder than promoting gigs. And you'll get a much better reward for your effort.

Show success before asking for help

I learned this huge life lesson from a secret document.

Music publishers give a cash advance to a songwriter in return for owning half the future income generated from their songs. The publisher is betting that those songs will earn at least as much as that cash advance.

I was working at Warner/Chappell music publishing, when someone stepped away from her desk. I noticed she had accidentally left out **the private financial statement showing every songwriter we had signed, the amount of their cash advance, and how much they had earned.** I secretly made a copy for myself, then put hers back.

I noticed a huge difference between two songwriters:

One was a great writer, constantly delivering songs with great hit potential, super professional, and a great collaborator. She got her deal because one of the managers heard her and believed in her. But she hadn't had any success yet.

Her advance: $15,000.

The other writer was horrible. His songs were really bad metal that would make the worst metal band cringe. They were poorly recorded and terribly performed. But in the 80s he had been in a band with a major rock star, so he had a partial songwriting credit on a song on a record that sold over 12 million copies.

His advance: $500,000.

The moral of this story?

You have to make your own success first, before you ask the industry for help.

Show that you're going to be successful without their help. Show that you have momentum. If they want to accelerate or amplify your success, they will have to pay to ride your train.

If you approach them before you can show some success, then you'll have no negotiating leverage, and will get the worst deal possible.

Test marketing

If you want a bigger company to help you some day, imitate what food companies call "test marketing".

When companies create a new product, before they try to release it to the world, they want more proof that it will be a success.

So first they'll release it only in a small city like Albany. They ask customers for feedback, then make improvements based on that. **They repeat this process until it's a local hit.** Then they test it in a few more small cities until it's a local hit there, too.

Only after it's a proven success do they get the financial backing to release it to the world. The investors are confident because it was a hit in all the test markets.

So think of what you're doing with your music as test marketing.

Whether you use a physical location or a virtual community, test it somewhere small first. Ask people for feedback, then make improvements based on that. Repeat this process until it's a local hit. Then test it in a few more places until it's a hit there, too.

Show this proof to a big company, so they can confidently invest and release it to the world.

Get rejected, get filtered

Have you heard of rejection therapy? It's a challenge—kind of a game—where you make it your mission to get rejected by someone every day. You have to do crazy things, like asking a stranger if you can try a bite of their sandwich. If they say no, you win for the day. The real point of the challenge is to overcome the fear of rejection by constantly exposing yourself to it.

Musicians usually send their music only to places that take everything. In other words: places that won't reject it. It's easier and feels better.

But think of the places that reject most music. Like media outlets, venues, and festivals. Like top professionals: successful agents, promoters, and producers. And ideally, places that usually don't have music at all.

If you look hard for them, you can find them, and do whatever it takes to get your music accepted by them. It takes more work, and you'll be rejected a lot. But you could approach it like rejection therapy.

Because once you get into any of these places, your credibility sets you apart from the rest, and opens more doors. You can even re-approach the places that rejected you before.

When you can show that you've made it through the filters—the places that weed out the bad music—it puts you in finer company: the best of the best.

Many more opportunities will open to you once you've earned your way through a few filters.

Be a competent novice, not an expert

Don't go too far down the rabbit hole of managing your little business.

It can become a brainless escape—a way to avoid the more open-hearted vulnerable work of making music. Updating your website instead of practicing. Answering emails instead of writing a new song.

Despite the fact that I talk so much about marketing, never forget that your music itself is always the most important thing. Unless your music is great, everything else is moot.

Get to the point of being a competent novice at business, then let an expert take it further.

If you sense you are becoming an expert, figure out what you love more. Maybe you're a better publicist than bassist. Maybe you're a better bassist than publicist.

Maybe it's time to admit your weakness as a booking agent, and hand it off to someone else. Maybe it's time to admit your genius as a booking agent, and commit to it full-time.

You can do anything, but you can't do everything. You have to decide.

Rock stars have a boss?

I was 20 years old. I had just moved to New York City. And I was working inside the music industry.

I ran the music library at Warner/Chappell. It was a huge room, near the executives' offices, and I had it all to myself.

Rock stars would come into my room before or after their meetings, to wait or relax. Because I was just some nobody working in the library, they would often speak candidly.

What surprised me was this: **These rock stars' biggest complaints were about the things they were forced to do, or not allowed to do!** Things like, "I think the album is perfect and finished, but the label says they don't hear a hit, so they're making me co-write." Or, "I wanted to make a video with this director I admire, but the label won't let me."

I had always assumed that rock stars were the top of the food chain. It was weird to realize they had a boss! **But that's the trade-off when you sign away your rights.**

The independent music revolution was so exciting because thousands of musicians were realizing that they didn't need to sign these kinds of deals anymore. They didn't need labels, distributors, publishers, or anything else to get their music to the public.

But years later, I still hear people making that trade-off. Giving up their rights and serving a company, in hopes of a greater reward.

- authors who act like Amazon is the boss

- web designers who act like Google is the boss

- promoters who act like Facebook is the boss

But you only have a boss if you choose to! Nobody is making you serve these masters.

Of course, if you don't want a boss, then everything is up to you. Less promotion, but more freedom. Less help, but keeping all your rights. Riding the back roads, not the highway. Serving no one but yourself.

Never forget you have the choice.

Resourceful

What it means to be resourceful

I was at a musicians' gathering in Memphis. I met a lot
of people complaining that their various forms of online
distribution weren't earning them as much as they'd hoped.

Then I met a musician who sold 8000 copies of his album
himself. No distributor. No website. Just by himself.

I asked him how he did it. He said, **"I just slowly drove
around the city every night, with the windows down,
playing my music loud. When I saw someone digging it, I'd
go talk with them. I'd sell almost everyone a copy—about
20 or 30 a night. Been doing this about a year. Sold 8000
so far."**

I love this story! It's so direct! It hit me especially hard
because all the musicians I'd met before him were
complaining about how it's impossible to make money
anymore.

It got me thinking about what it means to be resourceful.

The succinct way to show it is to contrast two different
mindsets. I'll call them A and B.

A: "I spent $60,000 making this album."
B: "I spent $60 making this album."

A: "There are no good live music venues anymore!"
B: "I made us a new venue."

A: "I've tried everything."
B: "I found a book from the 1970s with some unique
ideas I'm applying to our marketing."

A: "I don't have time to do it all!"
B: "Two of my fans help with promotion, one edits my videos, and one runs my website."

A: "I'm not some Hollywood networking dude. I don't have connections in the industry."
B: "My barber knew the promoter's wife, so it took some persistence, but now we're playing at his festival."

A: "They said we weren't allowed to just show up."
B: "We just showed up, and wouldn't leave. Eventually they said OK."

A: "We didn't get the festival gig."
B: "They rejected us, so we contacted every artist at the festival until we found one that insisted the promoter book us as their opening act."

A: "There's just no way!"
B: "I figured out a way."

It means being creative, rebellious, determined, and unstoppable.

It means asking for help, but not waiting for help.

You need to be profitable to last

A musician sent me her album, and very proudly said, "This cost $80,000 to make and two years to record. Everything is top-notch. We used one of the finest studios in the world."

She wanted me to be impressed, but once she said "$80,000" I lost hope in her ability to make a living making music.

I'd be much more impressed with someone who could make an album for $800, because that shows they are resourceful. They could record a hundred albums for the price of hers! If I was an investor, I'd invest in that kind of person.

Great music isn't enough. Losing money can't last. **For a career to be sustainable, it has to be profitable.**

Don't impress people with how much you spend. **Impress people with how little you spend.**

Same goes for expensive tools. The audience can't hear the difference between cheap and expensive equipment. So saying you need a certain tool is just another excuse to avoid the real work. The more talented somebody is, the less they need the props.

Your ability to be resourceful diminishes over time. You get older and feel you've earned the comforts. So especially early in your career, be as resourceful as possible. **It shows you can survive.**

Get specific!

This is one of the most useful lessons I've learned in life.

When you don't know your next step…
When you're feeling unmotivated…
When asking someone to help you…
When you're ready to make a dream come true…
Get more specific about what's needed.

There are two ways to do it:

#1: Write down every detail you know.

Inside your head, there is more than you've said. Take the time to write it all down.

When you have a vague or distant goal—like "be a great singer" or "make a million from my music"—break it down into specific ingredients. Describe concrete milestones, and exactly how to reach them. Then break those down into actions that you can start doing today.

When you're feeling stuck or unmotivated, figure out your next step. Even something as simple as finishing a song is easier when you realize exactly what's wrong.

When you hire someone to help you, write down absolutely everything you need them to do. Include every detail of every step, and your philosophy too.

#2: Research what you don't know.

Most people know what they want, but don't know how to get it. When you don't know the next step, you procrastinate or feel lost. But a little research can turn a vague desire into specific actions.

For example: When musicians say, "I need a booking agent", I ask, "Which one? What's their name?"

You can't act on a vague desire. But with an hour of research you could find the names of ten booking agents that work with ten artists you admire. Then you've got a list of the next ten people you need to contact.

A life coach told me that most of his job is just helping people get specific. Once they turn a vague goal into a list of specific steps, it's easy to take action.

It also makes you realize if something was a bad idea. Many things only sound nice in theory.

So do this for yourself. Take the time to get specific. It helps you and others to take action, and beats procrastination.

CALL THE DESTINATION, AND ASK FOR DIRECTIONS

Most of us don't know what to do next. We know where we want to be, but we don't know how to get there.

The solution is incredibly simple and effective:

Work backwards. Just **contact someone who's there, and ask how to get there.**

If you want to be in Rolling Stone magazine, call their main office in New York City. When the receptionist answers, say "Editorial, please." Ask someone in the editorial department which publicists they recommend. Then call each publicist, and ask how to become their client.

If you want to play a concert at the biggest club in town, show up on a weekday afternoon. Bring a box of pastries to the person that does the booking, and ask for just five minutes of their advice. Ask them what criteria must be met in order for them to take a chance on a new act. Ask what booking agents they recommend, or if they recommend using one at all. Keep your meeting as short as possible. Get the crucial info, then leave them alone until you're playing their club some day.

Call the destination, and ask for directions.

You'll get there much faster than walking without a map, hoping you arrive someday.

NEVER WAIT

One of the top music industry lawyers in Los Angeles was speaking at a conference.

She's an expert in copyright law, so someone asked her advice on a licensing problem. They had recorded their version of a famous song, but were unable to get the rights to sell it because they couldn't get a response from the publisher.

The lawyer shocked the audience when she said, "Sell it anyway. **Don't wait for permission.** Save the proof that you tried your best to reach them. If they contact you to ask for money some day, pay them then. But never wait."

Coming from a copyright lawyer, that was a bold statement.

It was a reminder that your career is more important than its details.

Success is your top priority. **Never let anything stop you.**

ASSUME NOBODY IS GOING
TO HELP YOU

I meet entrepreneurs who are waiting to find an investor. I meet musicians who are waiting to find a manager.

My advice is to assume nobody is coming. **It's more useful to assume that it's all up to you.** This is not hopeless, but helpful and empowering.

You probably heard about Aron Ralston, who got trapped in a remote canyon for five days and had to cut off his own arm to escape because he knew nobody would rescue him. They made a movie about it called "127 Hours". If he believed that someone would come, he would have just waited. But because he knew it was entirely up to him, he rescued himself.

When you assume nobody is going to help, you have to use all of your strength and resources. You can't wait, because there's nobody to wait for. **It keeps your focus on the things in your control—not outside circumstances.** It's productive pessimism.

Yes of course it's smart to always ask your fans and friends for help. Strive to work with the best collaborators, agents, producers, etc. But never count on their help. That's the difference.

Then, when someone does help you, it makes it even better.

The security of no security

If you're a full-time musician, you'll never have a job, a boss, a salary, or insurance. You'll bootstrap everything yourself. You'll always struggle against apathy and gate-keepers. And you'll have to be one-in-a-million to achieve this incredibly difficult goal.

To some people, this sounds horrible. To me, it was a dream come true.

Someone with a steady 9-5 job asked me how I could handle the lack of security.

Lack of security? **Living this way is like learning wilderness survival skills. Being able to fend for yourself is real security.**

- You're constantly thrown into new scenarios, and learn something new every time.

- You're not given a safety net, so you learn to make your own.

- Your career is not tied to any one company.

- Your success or failure is up to you—not the whims of a boss.

- You're a free agent, so you can take any opportunity.

- Your pay is always negotiable. You can experiment in doubling your rates, or charging however you'd like.

Basically, having no steady job keeps you at your best! To me, it's the ideal life.

A GOOD PLAN WINS NO MATTER WHAT HAPPENS

You don't need a formal business plan. But you do need a plan. **So make two simultaneous plans.**

Make one plan that depends on nobody else. No record deal. No investors. No lucky break. Your profits may be small but sustainable. Grow your audience. Develop your skills. Build your reputation. You can happily continue this way indefinitely.

Make another plan that uses the music industry. Build your team. Pursue a record deal. Find investors. Increase your odds of a lucky break.

Pursue these two plans simultaneously.

Then if a deal is offered to you, you can take it or leave it. It gives you great power in negotiation. You become a better investment when you don't need their money. It shows that you'll be successful whether they're involved or not.

If you're prepared for either path, then your plan wins no matter what happens.

Was 10%, now 90%

A few decades ago, as a musician, only 10% of your career was up to you.

A few gate-keepers controlled all the outlets. You had to impress one of these powerful people to be allowed to present your music to the world. So getting discovered was about all you could do.

But now 90% of your career is up to you. You have all the tools to make it happen.

You have to come up with a plan and make it happen. You have to make a great recording, a great show, a great video. You have to make thousands of people want your music so much they are willing to pay for it.

Record labels aren't guessing anymore. They're only signing artists that have built a success on their own. And even if a record label signs you, it's still up to you to make people want it!

The only thing stopping you from great success is yourself. This is both scary and exciting. But at least you're in control.

You don't get extreme results without extreme actions

You can't just normal your way through this.

Extreme talent requires extreme practice—training like an Olympic athlete.

Extreme success requires extreme focus—saying no to distractions and leisure.

Extreme fame requires extreme ambition—taking the spotlight and its pressure.

You can't do what everyone else does. You can't watch 63 hours of everyone's favorite TV show. You can't get two dogs that need you to be home. That's for normal people who want a normal life. That's not for you.

The music business is no place to be normal. The more intense, the better. Normal people will think you're insane. But your fellow achievers will welcome you to the exclusive club.

When you are not practicing, someone somewhere is practicing. And when you meet him, he will win.

Throw yourself into this entirely. **Find what you love and let it kill you.**

Direct it yourself

The "do it yourself" mentality is appealing. But it doesn't mean you do everything yourself. And it doesn't mean it has to be your hands.

Maybe at first, if you are just starting, and have no action, you can do everything yourself. It can be fun to make your website, engineer your recordings, design your artwork, book your gigs, and even play all the instruments when recording.

But as soon as you get momentum, you'll completely sabotage your success if you keep trying to do everything yourself.

Instead, learn to use others' hands. **Be like a film director. It's your vision. You decide how things are done.** You direct your team on what to do. You don't do everything yourself.

Yes, this means you need to find specialists at the other tasks. And yes, sometimes it's hard to find them. But it's harder to watch your career crawl instead of fly because you're trying to do it all yourself. I've seen too many make that mistake. Please don't.

Flip it in your favor

The old saying, **"It's all who you know,"** used to feel so defeating.

I wanted to be a famous musician, but I didn't know any famous people. I didn't grow up in Hollywood. None of my friends were successful. Fame was a secret insider's group.

So when I heard, "It's all who you know," it felt like the rest of that sentence was, "and you don't know anyone. So forget it."

One day in college we had a guest speaker who was a top executive at BMI.

On his way into class I overheard him say he was hungry. He had come straight to our school without lunch, so when the teacher told him it was a two-hour class, he groaned.

Because everyone was still getting seated, I quickly ran out to the hall, called the local pizza shop, and ordered a few pizzas to be sent to our classroom.

After they arrived, he laughed and said, "Good move. I owe you one." He gave me his card after class, and suggested I keep in touch.

For the next two years, he took my calls and gave me all kinds of advice about the music business. When I graduated college, he got me a great job at Warner/Chappell Music Publishing in New York City. He heard they were hiring, called them to say their search was done, and that was that. I started work that week.

A year later, I realized "It's all who you know," doesn't have to be depressing. I just never considered it could work in my favor.

Then I realized the profound conclusion. **Everything that seems depressing can be flipped to work in my favor.**

Every deal that's bad for someone is good for someone else. **So instead of moaning about the bad side, you can take the good side.**

If you think corporate radio is keeping your music from being heard, start a radio station! Look at the history of SomaFM.com for an example.

If you think banks have an unfair advantage, you can start a bank! Look at simple.com for an example.

In 1997, I thought distribution for musicians sucked. So I started CD Baby. Now distribution doesn't suck anymore.

If you live in a democracy and don't like the law, you can even change the law!

You can flip anything in your favor. It's easier than ever for you to replace a broken system, and never feel helpless again.

Not happy with existing venues? Make a new one

Gary Jules is a singer/songwriter from California. When he lived in Los Angeles he wished there was a venue more friendly to musicians. A place where people would come to listen, not talk over the music. A place to play, not showcase for labels.

Instead of complaining, he decided to do something about it.

He noticed a little coffee shop in a perfect location on Cahuenga Boulevard, but they had no music.

He asked if he could play there on Tuesday nights, and bring his own crowd and sound system. They let him.

Soon he was inviting his favorite artists as opening acts, and hosting a weekly songwriter's circle, too.

It was going well, so he left his PA system there full-time, and started booking great artists every night.

There was one big rule: no talking during playing. Audiences were warned not to talk, and performers would even stop the show if someone did. (Performers would say, "You can go anywhere else in LA to talk over the music. Not here.")

Within a couple months, the coffee shop didn't even open during the day anymore. It is now one of the best music venues in Hollywood, The Hotel Café, and world-famous artists play there every night.

To be clear: Gary did this in 2002. By the end of 2003, he had a #1 UK hit with the song "Mad World". The Hotel Café owners, Marko and Max, deserve all credit for the growth after that.

Anyway, the real point is not Gary or Hotel Café, but this:

If you're not happy with the way things are, don't just complain. Go make things how they should be.

DESCRIBE

When your music can't speak for itself

On the radio, your music speaks for itself. People hear your music and like it or not.

In concert, your music speaks for itself. Hearing and watching you perform is enough.

But in every other situation, unless your music is already in their ears, your music can't speak for itself. **The words that describe your music have to do the hard work.**

Online, the description needs to be so interesting that people stop to click and listen.

In word-of-mouth between friends, the description needs to be so memorable that people search for you later.

In the music industry, the description needs to be so intriguing that busy people feel you're worth their time.

These are the main ways you call attention to your music, so this is important.

Once you're a household name, and your music is playing everywhere, you can stop describing it. But for now, you need to come up with a great description.

A CURIOUS ANSWER TO THE MOST COMMON QUESTION

People will always and forever ask you, "What kind of music do you do?"

You will always and forever have to answer that question. So have a good description prepared in advance.

Many musicians avoid answering by saying, "We play all styles." No you don't. That's like saying, "I speak all languages."

Many musicians avoid answering by saying, "We are totally unique." No you're not. If you use notes, instruments, beats, or words, you're not totally unique.

If you give people a non-answer like this, you lose them. You had the chance to make a fan, and you blew it. They won't remember you because you gave them nothing to remember. You didn't make them curious.

Imagine if you had said, "We sound like the smell of fresh baked bread."

Or "We're the soundtrack to the final battle to save the earth."

Or "Bob Marley with a Turkish pipe smoking Japanese candy."

Then you've got their interest! A creative description also suggests that your music will be creative, too.

So make up a curious answer to that common question. You don't have to feel limited by it.

Notice that those three examples I gave could sound like anything. And that's the point.

With one interesting phrase to describe your music, you can make total strangers wonder about you.

But whatever you do, stay away from the words "everything", "nothing", "all styles", "totally unique", and the other non-answer: "a mix of rock, pop, jazz, hip-hop, folk, reggae, blues, techno, and metal."

Make people curious
in one sentence

Screenwriters in Hollywood constantly pitch their movie ideas to studio executives. Each one has about five seconds to impress. The one sentence they use to describe their story decides whether the studio will read it or not.

Same with you. You just need one good sentence to describe your music. It has only one goal: **Make people curious.** That's it.

It should not try to describe every note of music you make!

It should not try to justify your existence on Earth.

It only has to make them curious enough to listen. **That's all.**

I described my band as "a cross between James Brown and the Beatles". Of course not everything I did sounded like that, but that phrase was enough to make people want to hear it. I would watch them pause for a second to try to imagine what that might sound like. Then they'd say, "Wow—I have to hear this!" Mission accomplished.

The shorter, the better. Give them one good sentence and stop talking. Let them want to hear more.

WITHOUT A GOOD REASON,
THEY WON'T BOTHER

Someone sees you carrying a guitar and asks, "What kind of music do you play?"

You say, "There's no way to describe it. You just have to check it out. We're playing next Thursday night at 11. You should come."

Imagine reversing the situation:

You meet a man that says he's running a small business.

You ask what his company does. He says, "There's no way to describe it. You just have to check it out. We're open next Thursday for just one hour. You should come."

Would you really bother to go check out his business if he couldn't even tell you why you should? Of course not!

So how do you expect anyone to come hear you play?

You have to give people a good reason! Say a few words to make them curious.

When they ask what kind of music you do, they're actively hoping you'll give them a reason to care.

If you don't give them a reason in that very moment, the opportunity is gone.

Don't know how to describe your music?

Email everyone you know, saying you're trying to come up with a single phrase to describe your music, and ask their help.

Find a few teenagers, and treat them to pizza if they'll sit and listen to a few songs, then describe it for you while waiting for the pizza to arrive.

Hire a music writer to help you. This is what they do.

When you're playing on stage, ask people in the audience.

Read a music review site that describes music you've never heard. Notice which phrases make you curious to hear more.

When you've got one you like, try it out on people. See if their face lights up. **See if they get curious.**

When you've got a great description, you'll know it. Then you can use it for years and years.

Describe your music
like a non-musician

When describing your music, don't use musician language.

Don't say, "Wonderful harmonies and intricate arrangements. A tight rhythm section and introspective lyrics!" Real people don't understand what that means.

For most people, listening to music is like a cat watching cars go by.

"That's a fast one."

"That one was blue."

"Wow that was loud."

Only an expert or mechanic would be able to describe the technical details of the passing car.

So speak to people in their terms. Think what an office worker would say to a friend about your music: "It's cute! I love that song with the little 'hoop-hoop!' at the beginning, with that baby voice. It's kinda funky! And he's got this sexy bedroom voice. Cool video."

Think what one teenager at the skateboard park would say to another: "Dude, it's like if Kranetow hadn't wimped out. It's like Tweetown went metal, but they're from Mars or somethin'. It's slammin'. That chick's voice is insane!"

Real people will compare you to famous artists. Real people talk about the overall vibe or sound of something. Real people don't talk about "insightful lyrics", "strong melodies", or "tight musicianship".

Use their language.

USE THE TRICKS
THAT WORKED ON YOU

Find a media outlet that writes about new music.

You'll read about so many artists that you've never heard of before, and see their photos too.

Out of all of them, only one or two will really catch your attention.

Why? I don't have the answer. Only you do. **Ask yourself why a certain headline or photo or article caught your attention.**

Was it something about the opening sentence? Was it a curious tidbit about the singer's background? What was it exactly that intrigued you?

Analyze that. Use that. Adapt those techniques to write a headline or article about your music.

This also helps you get into the mindset of seeing yourself from others' point of view.

OR YOU CAN NOT TALK AT ALL

Maybe all these words have got you down, and you have nothing new to say?

Spend some money on a great photographer, and make a great video.

Plenty of sexy famous artists have proven that you don't have to talk and talk.

But if you don't, it's all up to the image, so your image better be really damn appealing.

HILLBILLY FLAMENCO

This is a story about how two words can change your career.

David and his band had always wanted to play at the big music festivals.

They had been performing at clubs for years, and doing pretty well, but he could never get the attention of the agents that book the festivals. He'd call them and submit his music, but those agents would never reply.

One night at a show, in between songs, a drunk fan shouted, "You know what you guys sound like? Hillbilly flamenco!" The crowd laughed, and so did the band. They joked about it on stage that night, and again on the drive home.

A week later, the band still remembered those two words: "hillbilly flamenco". It was funny, and the crowd liked it, and it actually described their music well. So they decided to use it more often.

Each time they played, they started telling the audience, "If you're wondering what kind of music this is, it's hillbilly flamenco!"

At the end of the show, they'd ask the audience, "When you tell your friends what kind of music you heard tonight, what will you say?" The crowd would shout, "hillbilly flamenco!"

And believe it or not, it worked! **People started telling their friends about this band, because it was so easy and fun to describe.** Attendance at their shows started going up and up.

Then one day, David once again called one of those agents who book the big festivals. But this time David said, "Our music style is hillbilly flamenco!"

The agent laughed and said, "Ok—I've got to hear this! I'm going to give you my personal address this time."

The agent finally listened to their music, and loved it. Now David and his band are playing the festivals they always wanted.

When he told me this story, he finished by saying, "Our career had a clear turning point. The day we started using those two words to describe our music, it made all the difference in the world."

TARGET

Aim for the edges

An amazing shift has happened in the last few decades.

You used to get successful by being normal and mainstream. But now you have a better chance of getting successful by being **remarkably unusual.**

Songwriters try to write a timeless standard that will resonate with everyone. But what good is that if nobody hears it because your music is too normal?

Our culture is now split into niches. In 1948, Milton Berle's TV show had 80% of all viewers, because it was one of only three choices! When the Beatles played on Ed Sullivan in 1964, they had 60% of all TV viewers. But now the biggest hit shows only get 1% of all viewers, because there are so many choices.

There won't be another blockbuster album like "Thriller" by Michael Jackson. With unlimited options now, music fans don't wait for mainstream media to tell them what to like. They can immediately listen to anything they want. Because of this, tastes are more spread-out than ever.

So reach the people who have headed to the edges. They're the ones who are looking for something new, and more likely to rave about it if you impress them.

Think of the metaphor of shooting an arrow at a bull's-eye target:

In the old blockbuster music business, you had a hit single or nothing. The only way you could be successful was to hit the exact center of a tiny distant target. If you missed the middle, you got nothing.

sive.rs/no-bullseye

Now it's like the target is closer and bigger, but there's a catch: Someone cut out the middle.

You can aim for the edge and hit something pretty easily. But if you're still aiming for the middle, there's nothing there.

So be remarkably unusual, and aim for those people who have headed to the edges.

IF YOU TARGET SHARP ENOUGH, YOU WILL OWN YOUR NICHE

Let's say you've decided that your style of music should be proudly called "power-pop".

- If you say, "We're power-pop!" in the very first sentence or paragraph all of your marketing.

- If your email address is "powerpop@gmail.com"

- If your album title is "Powerpop Drip and Drop"

- If the license plate on your band van is "POWRPOP"

When someone asks me for a music recommendation and says they like power-pop, guess who I'm going to tell them to buy?

Have the confidence to find your niche, define who you are, then declare it again and again and again and again.

If you do it persistently enough, you will own that niche. People will not be able to imagine that niche without you.

Don't forget you can **use your city or country** as a niche! Amplify your regional influence on your genre of music, and declare it to be an official sub-genre, of which you're the originator. Think of past examples: Minneapolis funk, Seattle grunge, Korean K-pop, Icelandic avant-garde, and of course the different kinds of hip hop from every corner of the world.

You can **make your own niche,** if you're brave. You might be the best "a cappella medieval metal" artist in the world.

Proudly exclude most people

We love when someone hates the same thing we hate—
especially if that thing is popular.

We're drawn to the confidence of someone who is not trying
to please anyone. We admire a strong, defiant stand.

You can use this to attract your future fans.

You can say, "If you like Katy Perry, you'll hate us." Then
people who hate Katy Perry will love that you said that and
want to check you out.

You can say, "Don't listen to this if you're happy with
your life." Then people who hate all that happy crap will
be intrigued.

Most musicians are trying to please everyone. So when you
are not, it suggests that you've got the talent to back up
your confidence.

You can be like the doorman of your exclusive club. Maybe
you refuse anyone who is over 30, or under 50. Maybe you
refuse anyone wearing a suit, or anyone without a tattoo.

There are some cool people around the world that would
like your music. They may only be 1% of the population. But
1% of the world is 75 million people!

Loudly reject 99%. It signals who you are. When someone in
your target 1% hears you proudly excluding the rest, they'll
be drawn to you.

Well-rounded doesn't cut

Imagine the world's attention as a big squishy pile of apathy—so thick you could cut it with a knife. To call attention to your music, you want to cut through that muck.

Only problem is, **if you're well-rounded, you can't cut through anything.** You need to be sharply defined, like a knife.

Let's look at a bad example first: Your name is Mary and you put out an album called "My Songs", and the cover is a picture of your face. The music is good quality, and the songs are about your life. When people ask what kind of music you do, you say "Oh, everything. All styles." You put your music out into the world but nothing much happens. Doors aren't opening.

Imagine instead: You write nine songs about food. You put out an album called "Sushi, Soufflé, and Seven Other Songs about Food". You recorded your vocals in the kitchen. You quit cooking school to be a musician. Now you've got an angle for promotion. Now people can remember and recommend it. Yes, it's a silly example, but you see how this would be much easier to promote?

You may be thinking, "But I have so much to offer the world, I can't just limit myself like that!" So stretch-out your musical offerings to the world over many years, and keep each phase focused clearly on one aspect of your music.

Look at the long careers of David Bowie, Miles Davis, Madonna, Prince, Joni Mitchell, or Paul Simon. Each went through sharply-defined phases, treating each album as a project with a narrow focus.

Be sharp as a knife, cut through the pile of apathy, and make a point.

Do this every year or two, and you will have a wide variety in the long run.

BE AN EXTREME CHARACTER

This is both fun and considerate.

When people say that a movie has a great character, they mean it was someone especially shocking, funny, or honest. To be a great entertainer, you need to be larger than life.

Push your outer boundaries. Show your weirdness. Bring out all your quirks. The world needs that.

Your public persona—the image you show the world— should be an extreme character. It can be a version of yourself, or it can be a mask. (It's easier to be honest behind a mask.)

Some of the biggest musicians of the last few decades have admitted they were playing a character. Eminem, for example, said he wrote lyrics with the goal of shocking a passive listener into paying attention. Then he built his public persona to match the lyrics.

Are you concerned that maybe you should play it safe, because your music isn't so extreme? Well... Think of the conservative, old-fashioned performers that your great-grandmother probably liked. Frank Sinatra. Judy Garland. Miles Davis. Billie Holiday. Even these old legends were rather extreme.

It's more interesting for the audience if you're the opposite of normal. So be an extreme character. The spotlight is the excuse. You can get away with anything in the name of entertainment.

A HUNDRED ACTORS ON STAGE

Imagine you're in the audience of a play, and there are a hundred actors on stage.

Which ones would stand out? Which ones would you remember?

It's not necessarily the loudest or most hyperactive. Maybe you'd be drawn to the woman with the long black hair, half-hidden, standing silently at the edge of the stage.

Now you, as a musician, are one of the actors on that over-crowded stage.

Would you stand out? **Would people know what you represent, at a glance?**

Be identifiable, so that people who want you can find you in the crowd.

(Though don't forget: the most memorable actor would be the one that talks with you after the show.)

The most expensive vodka

There is a vodka company that advertises itself as "the most expensive vodka you can buy".

It's enticing. It's almost a dare. (And it proudly excludes people!)

While most companies are trying to be the cheapest, a few do the opposite and aim to be the most expensive.

Most people try to imitate current trends and styles.
So I suggest you boldly declare that you are something totally un-trendy—the opposite of what everyone else is trying to be.

Advertise your live show as "the most boring concert you'll ever see."

Call your music "the most un-catchy, un-memorable, un-danceable music you've ever heard."

Tell the music industry "this music has no hit potential whatsoever."

I'll bet you get people's attention.

It's almost a dare.

Doing the opposite of everyone is valuable

It's supply and demand. **The more people do something, the less valuable it is.**

Everyone else is multi-tasking. So it's more valuable to single-task.

Everyone else is hyper-connected. So it's more valuable to disconnect.

Warren Buffett's investing advice is "Be fearful when others are greedy, and be greedy when others are fearful."

So do what others aren't doing.

If you play an instrument, give it a twist that nobody's done before. Like Greg Pattillo's beatbox flute. The New York Times said he's "the only person in the world who does what he does".

When I made a living playing colleges, I had three different acts: a rock band, a solo acoustic show, and "The Professional Pests", an act where I'd run around in a black lycra bag, bothering people. The Professional Pests out-booked the other acts by 5-to-1, because there are tons of rock bands, tons of solo acoustic shows, but only one place to hire a guy running around in a bag, bothering people.

Look at what your competitors are doing, then vow not to do that. **Don't try to beat them at their game. Play a completely different game.** Be radically opposite. Don't be associated with them in any way. Be so different that people don't even think to compare you.

Before Starbucks launched, a cup of coffee almost anywhere cost 50 cents. But Starbucks wanted to sell their coffee for $4. How could they get away with it? They made a unique ambience inside their shops. They created unique names for their sizes, like Grande and Venti. They created unique names for their drinks, like Frappuccino. Their offerings were so different that people accepted the $4 price without comparing it to the typical 50-cent cup of coffee.

That is how different you should be. Don't compete. Be completely different.

Selling music by solving a specific need

Instrumental music sells best if you tie it into a purpose.

Massage music sells very well.

Yoga music sells very well.

Instrumental Christmas music sells very well.

Notice they're selling more than just the music itself. They're selling something that non-music people find useful. **They solve a problem.**

Imagine two candlemakers.

One says, "My candles have only the finest wax with the best quality wick!"

The other says, "These are prayer candles. Light one whenever you pray."

There are dozens of people who will buy the first.

But there are millions who will buy the second.

People search harder for the obscure

On CD Baby, there was a great musician who made an amazing progressive heavy metal album.

When we had a "search keywords" section, asking for three artists he sounds like, he just wrote the biggest-selling pop acts of that time ("Britney Spears, Ricky Martin, Backstreet Boys").

What the hell was he thinking? He just wanted to turn up in people's search engines, at any cost. But for what? And who?

Did he really want a Britney Spears fan to get tricked into finding his dark progressive metal album? Would that pre-teen actually spend the time to listen to his ten-minute epic called "Confusing Mysteries of Hell"?

I suggested he instead have the confidence to target the real fans of his music.

So he put three obscure progressive metal artists into his search engine description. ("Fates Warning, Shadow Gallery, Angra")

And guess what? He sold more music than ever! People searching for these obscure artists found only him. He found his true fans.

Fans of the obscure niches search harder for it. Make sure they can find you. You want the passionate fans of your niche, not the casual fans of mainstream.

QUANTITY

Why you need a database

A database is just an organized collection of information. You could have a database of your music or your books. But I'm going to talk about a database of all the people you know.

Your email app is a kind of database. It has an address book of everyone you've emailed, and a history of your emails with each person. So you've already done half of what I'm going to describe here.

But I'm going to recommend you go further than that, and also keep track of:

- your private notes about people ("served in the army, loves talking politics")

- tags to help you find people ("drummer, programmer, agent")

- physical location ("London, England")

- when you should contact this person next ("3 weeks from today")

Once you have this information, you can easily find every agent you know in London, and email them about a gig.

Because the other best feature of a database is that it can personalize your communication. Instead of blasting out a message like "Hey everyone. How are you?", your database will send out personalized emails like, "Hey James. How are you?"—"Hey Sarah. How are you?". Not only does it get their attention better, but it's just more polite.

It will keep a history of your communication with everyone. This helps when you hear from someone for the first time in years. It can remind you who they are, and show you the last time you spoke. It also helps you do things like find just the people you haven't heard from in over a year. You can set calendar reminders, so it can remind you to follow-up with someone later.

As for which database to use, I have three recommendations:

1. Cloze. Go to Cloze.com. Link it with your existing inboxes and social media accounts, and it will pull in the information of everyone you've got in there already. It's brilliant and full of features.

2. Monica. Go to MonicaHQ.com. It's the most personal and people-focused, encouraging you to keep track of everything you know about everyone. It's also open source and free to install on your own server.

3. I ended up programming my own database software, which I plan to share for free some day. Maybe by the time you read this, it will be ready. Just email me to ask.

Using a database is one of the most powerful things you can do for your career. Please don't put it off. It's not as complicated as it sounds. The sooner you begin, the better.

Stay in touch with hundreds of people

Every person you've ever met has the potential to help you.

If you keep in touch and stay on their mind, there's a good chance an opportunity will come your way. But if you don't keep in touch, that potential is almost gone. Out of touch, out of mind.

So you need to make a simple automatic system to keep in touch without relying on your memory. Use your database to label everyone in a category like this:

- **A list:** Very important people.
  Contact every three weeks.

- **B list:** Important people.
  Contact every two months.

- **C list:** Most people.
  Contact every six months.

- **D list:** Demoted people.
  Contact once a year, to make sure you still have their correct info.

When you contact each person, just find out how they're doing. See if you can help them in any way.

This regular contact should be unselfish and sincerely caring. Don't ask a favor unless you've been in touch recently. It's a little insulting to contact someone you haven't talked with in a long time, just to ask a favor.

Most people are so bad at keeping in touch that they will really appreciate you doing it. And when you make this a habit, it's easy to stay in touch with hundreds or thousands of people.

Meet three new people every week

That's your simple goal to expand your network. Every single week, meet at least three new people that could help your career.

Have a real conversation—something more than text on a screen. Ask questions, get to know them, and make a personal connection. Learn what they're looking for, and how you can help them.

At this rate, you'll meet 150 new people each year. **The more people you know, the better.**

One of the biggest pop stars in the world right now got her start by meeting 50 people per day for a year! Before her first album, her manager took her around America, meeting every promoter, producer, radio director, video director, writer, editor, publisher—every person in the music business that could help her career. Just five minutes of hello, handshake, and "nice to meet you" with this charming future pop star. It must have been exhausting. But after a year of this, there were 15,000 people in the music industry that had met her face-to-face and will always feel a personal connection to her.

Though you probably won't go to this extreme, it's an example of how far you could take this idea.

If we assume your music is great, and you are a likeable person that people enjoy helping, I'll make this prediction: **The number of people you meet will determine your success.**

Keep in touch

When I was promoting myself as a musician, I noticed an interesting pattern. If I had a good conversation with somebody in the music business, then quite often they would send an opportunity my way within a day or two.

In other words, when I look back at the random opportunities that came my way, they often came from someone who I had just spoken with a day or two before.

Yes I just said this twice to emphasize it. This is important.

Years later, when I was running CD Baby, various opportunities came up where someone asked me to recommend a musician. I almost always recommended whichever musician I had just spoken with, since they came to mind first. That's why it's so important to keep in touch.

There were some amazing musicians whose music I loved, so I contacted them to tell them I'm a huge fan, and would love to help however I can. But if they didn't keep in touch, they eventually fell out of my mind. It's unfortunate, but that's life.

There were some good (but not amazing) musicians who were great at keeping in touch. So when opportunities came my way, guess who I thought of to recommend? Yep. That's life.

The difference between success and failure can be as simple as keeping in touch.

It takes effort to meet people. So once you've met someone, get the most out of the relationship for both of you. Keep in touch.

Every breakthrough comes from someone you know

When I was promoting my music, I used to look to the big wide world for opportunities.

Only later, I realized that every great thing that happened in my career came from someone I knew.

When you come to an opportunity through a connection, you have an advantage. You're not anonymous. You've already passed through a filter, and passed a test. You're special because it's a personal referral.

Does this mean you should stop looking to the world for opportunities? No! Of course not!

Take some of that searching time, and spend it on keeping in touch with your existing contacts.

Then also keep looking to the world. But when you find an opportunity, don't just toss your music in with the rest. Get to know the people behind it. Set yourself apart. Get personal. **And now this is someone you know.**

Every breakthrough comes from someone you know.

Put your fans to work

You know that guy who comes to all your shows?

You know that woman who tells you how much she loves your music?

You know that fan who said, "If you ever need anything, just ask!"?

Put them to work!

People who reach out like that are looking for a better mission—a connection to your world. You might be the coolest thing that ever happened to a teenager going through an unpopular phase. You might help someone start a new life after a break-up. You can provide some exciting variety to their boring routines.

Write out a list of what needs to be done. Invite them over for pizza to spend an evening helping. Hit the town together, posting concert flyers. Ask them to go through a list of media outlets and contact five people per week.

You might think, "How could anyone want to do this boring work for free?" But many people have too much time on their hands, and want to spend it on something besides TV.

To most people, the music business is pure magic. It's rebellion and passion and fantastically romantic. They can live vicariously through someone following their passionate dreams against all odds.

Working with you might be the closest they get to that magical world. Give someone the chance to be on the inside circle. Put them to work.

Include everyone in your success

Everyone who is drawn to you before you're famous is thinking the same thing: **You might be famous soon!**

- fans who want to help you

- professionals who want to meet you

- musicians who want to play with you

- companies that want to work with you

They're all hoping to be included in your glorious future.

As you get more successful, share that success with those who helped you years ago. When you're in the tornado of fame, you can't depend on your memory. So use your database now to keep track of who has done special favors for you. **When you are famous, return the favors.** Reach out to contact them, and invite them into your new world. (Don't wait for them to ask.)

Those who gave their services for free? Now you can pay full price.

Those who wanted glamour by association? Invite them to the best party.

Those who deserve more recognition? Shout their praises to your new audience.

You aren't pulled to success by destiny. You're lifted there by those around you. So acknowledge their contribution, and bring them along for the ride.

How to attend a conference

Attending a music conference is the most efficient way to meet the most number of the best contacts.

People who attend conferences are ambitious, working in the industry now, and open to meeting new people.

I highly recommend you go to a few music industry conferences every year.

That said… **Most people completely waste their time and money when they attend a conference.** So here's how to do it right:

Get interested and listen.

You know the way to be interesting to others is to **be interested** in them.

So the week before the conference, read one or two books about **how to be a great listener.** (The original classic from the 1930s is titled "How to Win Friends and Influence People" but there are many similar books about people skills, and they're all good.)

Then use the conference as your testing ground for your new listening skills. Get extremely interested in those around you. Think like an investigative reporter.

For each person you meet, think about how you can help them.

Turn to a stranger and say, "Hi. What do you do?"

Ask how they got into that. Ask what's hard about it. Figure out how you can help them.

If they're too shy, help by introducing them to the next person you meet and inviting them to dinner. If they're too popular, help them escape the crowd for a little peace and quiet.

Trade contact info within a few minutes of meeting. If you wait too long, one of you will get pulled away, and it will be too late.

If you're an introvert like me, this will be exhausting. But you only need to do it for a few hours, and this only happens a few times per year. It's worth the effort.

Each night, before bed, enter everyone's info into your database, including your private notes on what you remember about each person. It's crucial to do this before you meet more people the next day.

Send them a message immediately, connecting the digital you to the physical you. ("Hi John. Good to meet you today. You were right about the bicycles! Here's a link to that site you asked about. See you at the closing party tomorrow.") Include your full contact info.

By being sincerely interested in them and actively trying to help them, they will probably be interested in you and try to help you.

WHAT ABOUT YOU?

Notice I said nothing about promoting yourself. This is about them, not you. Your promotion will come later.

People will ask what you do. **Don't give a boring answer—it's rude.** If you say "I'm a bassist", then they'll say "oh", followed by awkward silence and an excuse about why they need to walk away now.

Before the conference, come up with one interesting sentence that says what you do—including a curious bit that will make them ask a follow-up question. For example: "Bassist of the Crunchy Frogs—the worst punk bluegrass band ever. We're headlining the showcase tonight. Our singer is a pirate." See how that would lead to questions? Anyone who hears that will ask you why you are the worst, or why your singer is a pirate. You're helping them engage in a conversation! Also, by quickly mentioning an accolade, you're showing them you're worth knowing.

But please stop after you say your sentence. **The only thing worse than a short boring answer is a long boring answer.** Leave room for them to ask something! If they don't, change the subject back to them.

Don't push your stuff on someone who isn't asking for it. It's the biggest turn-off of all. Because it shows you don't understand the real point, which is…

REAL BUSINESS IS DONE IN THE FOLLOW-UP, NOT THE CONFERENCE ITSELF.

The conference itself is a mad blitz of distractions. Only use it for these initial connections.

Assume that anything you hand someone at a conference will be thrown out. So don't do it, unless they ask.

Instead, if you want them to have something of yours, send it to them later.

The best time to get down to business is when they're **alone, back at their office, a week or two after the conference**, and can give you their full one-on-one attention.

That's when you want someone to check out what you have to offer: when they're focused on you.

They'll remember you as very interesting. Then they'll find out you're also very talented.

IT'S ALL ABOUT THE FOLLOW-UP.

After attending over a hundred conferences in twenty years, I can tell you from experience that only about 1% of the people ever follow up. Therefore, 99% of them wasted their time and money. Please don't be in that 99%.

Everything happens in the follow-up. Remember this, and you'll do well.

Don't be a mosquito

A mosquito enters a room of people only to suck something out of them.

People hate mosquitos.

It's important to meet people, but more important to get to know them. Ask questions. Listen.

Learn what they love. Learn what they want. **Figure out what you can do for them.**

Relationships are reciprocal. You need to give to receive.

Don't be a mosquito.

MONEY

SHED YOUR MONEY TABOOS

Everyone has weird mental associations with money.

They think the only way to make money is to take it away from others. They think that charging for your art means it was insincere, and only for profit.

But after knowing thousands of musicians for over twenty years, I've learned this:

The unhappiest musicians are the ones who avoided the subject of money, and are now broke or need a draining day job. It may sound cool to say money doesn't matter—to say "don't worry about it!"—but it leads to a really hard life. Then ultimately your music suffers, because you can't give it the time it needs, and you haven't found an audience that values it.

The happiest musicians are the ones who develop their value, and confidently charge a high price. There's a deep satisfaction when you know how valuable you are, and the world agrees. Then it reinforces itself, because you can focus on being the best artist you can be, since you've found an audience that rewards you for it.

So never underestimate the importance of making money. Let go of any taboos you have about it.

Money is nothing more than a neutral exchange of value. If people give you money, it's proof that you're giving them something valuable in return.

By focusing on making money with your music, you're making sure it's valuable to others, not only to you.

Valuable to others, or only you?

When I'm hot, it's hard for me to imagine that others in the room are cold. I think it really *is* hot, not that it's hot only for me. It feels like a fact, not an opinion.

When I do something that's really valuable to me, it's hard for me to imagine that it's not valuable to others. I think it really *is* valuable, not that it's valuable only for me. It feels like a fact, not an opinion.

This is understandable. Our feelings feel like facts. It's hard to imagine that they're not.

This is the problem of the "starving artist".

When someone creates something that feels important, powerful, and valuable to them, it's hard to imagine that it's not important, powerful, and valuable to others.

But money only comes from doing something valuable to others.

The starving artist pours his heart into a project that's incredibly valuable to him, but not (yet) valuable to others. That's why no money comes.

The good news is **there are two ways out of the starving artist problem,** and either one can be fun.

#1: Focus on making your music more valuable to others.

Art doesn't end at the edge of the canvas. Keep your creativity going. Constantly ask, "How can I be more valuable to an audience?" You may come up with ideas like this:

- Convert what you do from a public display to a personal service. Customize your work for hire.

- Spread a fascinating version of your history, so fans can get emotionally interested in you.

- Be more entertaining, so that people don't need sophisticated tastes to appreciate your music.

- Make your shows invitation-only.

- Engage more senses. Make a live performance so visually interesting that even deaf people would love it. Can you even incorporate smell, touch, or taste?

- Go where money is already flowing. Adapt what you do to match the needs of businesses, holiday resorts, hospitals, or universities.

Then force yourself to try all the best ideas, even if it seems unnatural at first. Read books about business and psychology to get more ideas, since many brilliant minds are asking the same question from a different perspective.

Do this repeatedly, paying attention to feedback from others, and you will become more valuable.

Though if you find that this makes you more miserable than excited, try the other way:

#2: STOP EXPECTING IT TO BE VALUABLE TO OTHERS.

Accept your music as personal and precious to only you. Get your money elsewhere.

Sex with my girlfriend is very valuable to me and her, but luckily I'm not trying to make it valuable to others.

If you stop expecting your music to be valuable to anyone but you, your conflicted mind can finally be at peace. Do it only because you love it, and it honestly doesn't matter what anyone else thinks.

You might even keep it private like a diary, just to be clear who it's really for.

You'll probably be happier with your music because of this change in mindset. Ironically, others may appreciate it more, too, though you honestly won't care.

Pricing philosophy

For years I made a living playing at universities.

One time a college far away in Ohio—about a 12-hour drive—asked what I would charge to do a **two-hour show.**

I said, "$1500".

She said, "Oh, that's a bit too much. What would you charge to do just a **one-hour show?"**

I said, "$2000".

She said, "No, wait, you'll be performing less, not more!"

I said, "Yeah! Exactly! What you're paying me for is to get there! Once I'm there, playing music is the fun part! If you tell me I have to get back in the van and drive home after only an hour, then I'm going to charge you more than if you let me play for a couple hours first."

She liked that so much that she came up with the $1500.

Point is: Business is creative. You can do things any way you want. There's no need to adhere to norms. Norms are for businesses without personality.

Pour your personality and philosophy into the way you do business. People actually appreciate it when you do things in a surprising way. It shows you care more than most—that you're putting your self into this—that you're not just in it for the money.

Emphasize meaning over price

A musician named Griffin House used to sell CDs at his gigs for $15. He'd mention it once or twice from the stage, and sell about **$300 per night on average.**

One day his manager, Terry McBride, asked him to try a completely different approach. He said:

Tell the audience, "It's really important to us that you have our CD. We worked so hard on it and are so proud of it, that we want you to have it, no matter what. Pay what you want, but even if you have no money, please take one tonight."

Say this again before the end of the show. "Please, nobody leave here tonight without getting a copy of our CD. We've shared this great show together so it would mean a lot to us if you'd take one."

It changes the request from a commercial pitch to an emotional connection. Allowing them to get a CD for no money just reinforces that.

As soon as Griffin made this change, he started selling about **$1200 per night on average,** even including those people who took it for free! The average selling price was about $10.

But the important part came next:

Because every person left each show with a CD, they were more likely to remember who they saw, tell friends about it, listen to it later, and become an even bigger fan afterwards.

Then, when the band returned to a town where they had insisted that everyone take a CD, **attendance at those shows doubled!** The people that took a CD became long-term fans and brought their friends to future shows.

So, whatever you're selling, emphasize the meaning of it, not the price.

SOME PEOPLE LIKE TO PAY. LET THEM

Not everyone is broke.

When musicians put me on the guest list at a venue, I pay anyway. I like to support the venue and the artist.

When the record label Magnatune let people pay as little as $5 to buy an album, they paid an average of $9.82. Many pay much more, because they know it goes to the artist.

Radiohead's album "In Rainbows" was offered for free, but 40% of people chose to pay for it anyway.

It's like donating money to their favorite charity. They don't have to, but it makes them happy.

When you're offering something for free, don't forget that there are lots of people that like to pay! **Appeal to this side of people, giving them a reason to pay that feels good.**

Tell them what their payment will support. Show them how much you appreciate the purchase. It will actually make them happy to give you money.

THE HIGHER THE PRICE, THE MORE THEY VALUE IT

Psychology experiments have shown that the more people pay for something, the more they value it.

People given a placebo pill were twice as likely to have their pain disappear when they were told that the pill was expensive.

People who paid more for tickets were more likely to attend the performance.

When people want the best, they look to the price to tell them what's great. They think the expensive wine tastes better. They think the expensive headphones sound better. Even when secretly, those things are no different than the cheap ones.

If you sign a deal with a company, negotiate the biggest up-front advance possible. Even if you don't need the money, it's the best strategy, because the higher your advance, the harder the company will work to earn it back. It ends up being better for everyone.

Tony Robbins, back when he was first getting successful, started charging one million dollars for personal consultations. His reason was surprising. It wasn't for the money. It was because his goal was to help people improve their life, and his biggest problem was people not doing the necessary work after coming to see him. So if someone spends a million dollars, they're sure as hell going to do the work. He says it kept his success rate at 100%.

So it's considerate to charge more for your work. People will appreciate it more, and get better results.

ARE FANS TELLING FRIENDS?
IF NOT, DON'T PROMOTE

Should you spend more time promoting right now?

Or should you spend more time creating and improving?

It's a tough question. Lucky for you, I've got the answer.

It comes down to one observation: **Are your fans telling their friends?**

If not, then don't waste time promoting it yet. Keep working, improving, and creating, until your fans are telling their friends about you.

To be clear, I don't mean fans told friends because you asked them to! They can't do it just to help you, like a favor. They have to do it just because they love your music so much that they're doing their friends a favor by turning them on to you.

Your music needs to be remarkable—so surprisingly good that others remark about it, like this.

Until that point, you're better off just improving and creating as much as you can.

For more thoughts on this, read Seth Godin's book, "Purple Cow".

Don't promote until people can take action

I often hear musicians say they want to do advance promotion—telling people about their new album before it's available for purchase.

Though the plan may be to generate excitement, I think the opposite happens. Imagine the dialogue.

"Check out my new music!"

"Where is it? Can I buy it?"

"Not yet—but soon!"

"Why are you telling me now?"

"So you can be ready for the announcement!"

(Then two months pass.)

"Check out my new music! It's ready!"

"I think I already heard of this. Not new. Delete."

Instead, imagine this plan:

1. Record your music.

2. Start conversations with the people who promote music. Don't pitch them anything. Just get to know them.

3. Prepare your marketing plan, but don't do it yet. Just get everything into place.

4. Get your music distributed everywhere. Before you announce it, make sure it's actually there. Stream and even buy a copy, to make sure there were no mistakes.

5. Finally, do your promotion, and tell everyone.

One of the nice things about crowd-funding is that for each project, there are two stages when people can take action, so you can repeat this cycle twice.

Never promote something until people can take action, or you might waste the one moment you had their attention.

Never have a limit on your income

Imagine two people. One is a toy maker. One is a masseuse.

Imagine both get suddenly famous. Now a million people want that toy. And a million people want a massage from that masseuse.

For the toy maker, that's no problem. Have the manufacturer make a million more.

For the masseuse? That's a big problem. She's limited by her hands-on time.

So which business would you rather be in? One that makes money while you do other things, or one that only profits by your own two hands?

Many pundits say that since people aren't buying recorded music, musicians should just be in the business of playing concerts. You can see the flaw in that plan. It limits your income.

So what other ways can your music earn income while you sleep? Originally I had a list of ideas here, but they were all really obvious, and I don't know what decade it will be by the time you read this. So the important thing is to keep asking the question, and keep trying the ideas.

Mindset

MOVE TO THE BIG CITY

I hate to admit this, but it's true.

One of the best things you can do for your career is to move to a big city—one of the major media centers—the places that broadcast to the entire world. **Nothing less than New York, Los Angeles, London, Mumbai, Hong Kong, or maybe San Francisco.** (Nashville, Paris, Seoul, or Tokyo only count if you're limiting yourself to those markets.)

It's the place where everything happens. Where the biggest media companies in the world are based. Where the money is flowing. Where the most successful agents, producers, and executives live and work. Where the most ambitious people go.

It has a serious energy, because the stakes are high. It's not casual. It's not a place for a comfortable work/life balance. It's fueled by ambition. People go go go.

I've lived in a bunch of places now, but when I look back at my career, it's obvious that the biggest breakthroughs happened because I was living in the heart of the music industry in New York and Los Angeles.

It shows that you're in the game. It shows you're serious. It gives you healthy competition, knowing that today's biggest stars and legends are there with you, too. It challenges you to push your skills to the best of the best, instead of just the best in your home town.

Once you're famous, and the media is carrying your reputation, you can move away if you want. But even then you'll be a little out of the game. You can decide if that's OK with you.

I lived in New York City for nine years, and Los Angeles for seven years. I met so many wonderful kindreds—other ambitious people like me that had moved there from around the world to get successful.

So why do I hate to admit this?

Because I love how the internet has made it possible for anyone to get successful, anywhere. I love the idea of living in the middle of nowhere, surrounded by nature, yet being connected to the world.

But still, when I look at the facts, it's impossible to deny. **Living in the big city, and being where everything is happening, will help your career the most.** Being anywhere else won't hurt you, but it won't help.

Detailed dreams blind you to new means

There's a fable of a man stuck in a flood. Convinced that God is going to save him, he says no to a passing canoe, boat, and helicopter that offer to help. He dies, and in heaven asks God why He didn't save him. God says, "I sent you a canoe, a boat, and a helicopter!"

We all have vivid imaginations. We get a goal in our mind and picture the path so clearly. Then it's hard to stop focusing on that vivid image, to see what else could work.

New technologies make old things easier, and new things possible. **That's why you need to re-evaluate your old dreams to see if new means have come along.**

Some actors move to Hollywood hoping to get noticed. Others use every new outlet to make themselves unavoidable.

Some authors are just waiting for a publisher to sign them. Others are getting rich just self-publishing.

You need to distinguish between your real goal and the unnecessary details. **Don't let the details distract you from your goal.**

For each of your dreams, occasionally ask yourself what the real point is. Then look for a better way to get to that point.

Let go of outdated dreams that keep you from noticing what's here now.

ARE YOU AT THE STARTING LINE OR THE FINISH LINE?

New clients would often ask me, "How much does the average artist on CD Baby sell?"

Some people would take our posted sales figures and divide them. $85 million paid, divided by 250,000 available albums = $340 per album.

The numbers are right but the answer is wrong because it groups together two completely different approaches.

For some artists, releasing their music is like the starting line in a race. The gun goes off! They work it! They spend hours a day pushing, promoting, and selling—reaching new people by any means necessary.

For those types the average income, through my one little store, was $5000. Fifty of them earned over $100,000 each.

But for many artists, releasing their music is like the finish line in a race. They've always wanted to record and release their music. They did it. It's done. They send it to friends and family, and glow in the compliments. Their efforts are basically finished—either because they're satisfied, or because they assumed the world would just flock to it automatically.

For those types the average income was $20.

New clients who asked about the average were trying to predict how well they would sell. But it depends on which approach you want to take.

Are you at the starting line or the finish line?

That's the best predictor of how far you'll go.

Nobody knows the future, so focus on what doesn't change

At every music conference, with a panel of experts on stage, the moderator always asks, "What's the future of the music business?"

The guy selling video subscriptions will say that videos are the future.

The guy selling intelligent playlists will say that intelligent playlists are the future.

When they ask me, I always say, "Nobody knows the future, and anyone who pretends to know can't be trusted."

We have a desperate need for certainty, so we want someone to tell us what's coming. But it's impossible. Nobody can possibly know.

Besides, would it matter what anyone says? Realistically, what would you change about what you're doing, day-to-day? Like if someone said, "Scented holograms are the future", would you start making them tomorrow? No.

Instead, forget predicting, and focus on what doesn't change. Just like we know there will be gravity, and water will be wet, we know some things stay the same.

People always love a memorable melody. You can't know what instrumentation or production style will be in fashion. So focus on the craft of making great melodies.

People always want an emotional connection. You can't know what technology will carry that communication. So focus on the essence of how to connect with an audience.

Writing lots of songs increases your chances of writing a hit. You can't know which song will be a hit. So write as many songs as you can.

Instead of predicting the future, focus your time and energy on the fundamentals. The unpredictable changes around them are just the details.

Ignore advice that drains you

My music career was derailed when I took some advice from an expert.

When my own music was at its peak success, a famous lawyer said he wanted to work with me. He said I should start a label, sign a few other artists, make them successful too. Then instead of getting me a simple artist deal, he could help me get a deal for the entire label for over a million dollars.

I walked out of his office sad, but acknowledging that he was right. **That was the smartest thing to do to be a big success.** So that's what I did. I stopped putting my full attention into my own music, and tried to sign and produce other artists.

I spent two long years on this. **But the whole time, I hated it!** I only loved my own music. I only wanted to be an artist, not a label.

So, as you can imagine, it didn't go well. My label was a failure, and my own music career lost momentum because I lost focus.

I wish I had paid attention to my emotions, and not wasted years of my life following someone's advice.

Point is: You're going to hear a lot of advice. Listen to it all, but pay close attention to what it does to your energy and focus. **If it makes you jump into action, it's good advice. If it makes you feel drained, sad, or lost, then it's not for you.**

COMPASS IN YOUR GUT

Your instincts have a compass that points two directions:

1. what excites you

2. what drains you

No matter what advice anyone gives you—no matter how smart they may be—you need to let this compass guide you.

Whatever excites you, go do it.

Whatever drains you, stop doing it.

For example: Many musicians get into music because they love playing their instrument. They love it so much they want to do it full-time. But then well-meaning people say, "If you're going to be in the music business, you have to read this book on music business law, and you have to learn networking skills, and marketing, and tech skills, and accounting, and writing good newsletters, and blah blah blah." Soon those musicians are spending all their time doing everything but playing their instrument, and decide it's not worth it! They give up, get a dumb job, and lose interest in their instrument, because a career in music seems tedious and overwhelming.

But nothing is worth losing your enthusiasm. Nothing!

Whatever excites you, go do it. Whatever drains you, stop doing it. You have to pay close attention to that compass, even in little day-to-day decisions.

You get offered a gig. They're on the phone waiting for an answer. Does it excite you or drain you?

You hear about some new technology. People say you need to check out this new app. Does it excite you or drain you?

If it doesn't excite you, don't do it. **There's almost nothing that you *must* do.**

Whatever you hate doing, someone out there loves doing it. So if it's necessary, find them and let them do it.

Work toward this ideal, and soon you'll be doing only what excites you the most.

Then you'll find that doors open for you, opportunities come your way, and life seems to go easier, because you're doing what you're meant to do.

ABOUT THE AUTHOR

If you want to know more about me or my work, go to **sive.rs.** It's all there.

Anyone who reads my books is my kind of person, so please go to **sive.rs/contact** to email me and say hello. Ask me anything, or just introduce yourself. I read and reply to every email.

—Derek